Calculated Blessings

EVERY TEAR COUNTS

EVANGELA C. W. JEFFREY

ISBN 978-1-63844-473-2 (paperback)
ISBN 978-1-63844-474-9 (digital)

Christian Faith Publishing, Inc.
832 Park Avenue
Meadville, PA 16335
www.christianfaithpublishing.com

Printed in the United States of America

To those who are wearing the uniform of
hurt, disappointment, or shame,
wipe your tears, and change your clothes!

Turn again, and tell Hezekiah the captain of my
people, Thus saith the LORD, the God of David
thy father, I have heard thy prayer, I have seen
thy tears: behold, I will heal thee: on the third
day thou shalt go up unto the house of the LORD.
(2 Kings 20:5)

Thou tellest my wanderings: put thou my tears
into thy bottle: are they not in thy book? (Psalm
56:8)

I am weary with my groaning, all the night make
I my bed to swim, I water my couch with my
tears. (Psalm 6:6)

They that sow in tears shall reap in joy. (Psalm
126:5)

And straightway the father of the child cried out,
and said with tears, Lord, I believe, help thou
mine unbelief. (Mark 9:24)

For the Lamb which is in the midst of the throne
shall feed them, and shall lead them unto the
fountains of waters: and God shall wipe away all
tears from their eyes. (Revelation 7:17)

This book is dedicated to four groups of people who have affected my life in a most profound way.

To the Holy Trinity;, because of You, I live and move and have my being. You are my protector, my guide, my healer, my provider, my everything…

To my friends, I can only hope and pray that I have been as good of a friend to you as you have been to me: …inspirational, loving, and supportive among other things…

To my family, especially my daughter and her crew;, Mr. J. (was not the man of my dreams but certainly turned out to be my knight in shining armor—, my prince charming);, my mother;, my father, who fell asleep in April 2014;, my siblings;, and my aunts and uncles;, my cousins;, my nieces;, and my nephews…there are so many that I dare not begin to name them one by one lests I forget one or run out of paper, but please know that I love each and every one of you.

To my former Pastor, Reverend Jim Charles Foster, who has fallen asleep, you will always remain in my thoughts and in my heart. I thank you for your wisdom and knowledge and obedience to the Word. To my current Pastor, Bishop C. Anthony Muse, and Elder, Lady Pat Lawson Muse, who are alive, well, and love the Lord! I love you and I thank God daily for the gifts and talents, and love that He has placed in you that you impart into the Ark of Safety Christian Church—; members, guests, affiliates, and visitors alike. If you are ever in the Upper Marlboro area of Maryland, stop by the Ark of Safety Christian Church for a visit.

Contents

Foreword 9

Chapter 1: It's Not Punishment But A Process 11
Chapter 2: Try Him Before You Deny Him 13
Chapter 3: My Condition Is Not My Conclusion 15
Chapter 4: The Numbers Don't Add Up 17
Chapter 5: We Can't Work It Out 19
Chapter 6: Calling All Angels 21
Chapter 7: To Get One, Be One 23
Chapter 8: A Way With Words 24
Chapter 9: You Can't Tell Everybody Everything 26
Chapter 10: Dress For Success 28
Chapter 11: Don't Faint 30
Chapter 12: Before I Let Go 32
Chapter 13: Faith Don't Fail Me Now 34
Chapter 14: Safety In The Ark 36
Chapter 15: Who Can I Run To? 38
Chapter 16: Forgive Or Relive 40
Chapter 17: Prayer Still Works 42
Chapter 18: Keep The Testimony 44
Chapter 19: Attitude Of Gratitude 46
Chapter 20: What's Next? 48

Foreword

First, I'm giving honor to God, from whom all blessings flow. I love him so much. He has truly been good to me. He allows me to rise each morning, and not only that, he gives me gifts when I awaken, a new set of mercies. I thank him for a new set every morning because the mercies that he granted me yesterday…let's just say that they are not like the unused minutes on your cell phone: they never roll over.

This book is one that I have dreamed of writing for some time now. It is a compilation of a few of my thoughts that I wanted to put on paper. As mentioned, I have wanted to do this for a long while but was held captive by fear. What would people say? What would they think? I have never been known as one who procrastinates, but fear, in this instance, may be viewed as a form of procrastination. Fear is a terrible thing, and having carried it for a while, I feel that it is such a relief to finally and truthfully be able to tell you today that a burden has been lifted. I am restored, and now, I am free to move on to the next thing. But as a good friend once told me, "Nothing happens before its time."

I really wanted this book to be a *just-as-I-am* project, so at first, I did not get too bogged down with the proofreading and other steps that would normally take place in the publishing process. I do believe in order, but I also believe that one should have the freedom to explore different paths for getting things done and to explore different forms of expression. I have come to the revelation that I am not perfect, though I do strive for excellence, and that I needed assistance with this. So I decided to secure an awesome publishing company that was very hands-on in helping catapult my dream to reality. Prayerfully, this book will help someone else to get over their fear and pull their dream into reality, realizing that we all make mistakes but that the joy of living is being able to get up, dust yourself off, and keep it moving.

CHAPTER

It's Not Punishment But A Process

For his anger endureth but for a moment; in his favour is life: weeping may endure for a night, but joy cometh in the morning.

—Psalm 30:5

I used to ask myself, "Why me, Lord? Why me?" Now, I have come to understand that, if you truly trust God and put forth an effort to earnestly walk in his will and his way, as it is written in Isaiah 54:17, "No weapon that is formed against thee shall prosper." I have also come to realize that there are times when one becomes his own stumbling block. Life is simply a "muscle-building" journey, a strengthening exercise. If one never adds more weight, he will never know his limits or just how strong he can become—how much he can endure. Everything happens for a reason.

We are often tested and tried, but maybe that is our purpose in life: to be examples, to be able to help someone else through a situation. "Hey, look at me or, better yet, look at the God in me." Situations are our opportunities to walk in our discipleship. When we encounter—and the Holy Spirit will lead us to people who are going through things that we have conquered—people who are on the verge of giving up, thinking that it is over and that there is no way out, we can speak into their lives, "I have been there. There is hope. You have tried it your way, now let me show you God's way." This act can save someone's life and ultimately lead them to Christ.

I am reminded of the life and determination of Paul, how, after his experience on the road to Damascus, the course of his life was dramatically changed. Paul described himself as an "ambassador for Christ." Even in his chains, he was determined to strengthen others in the joy and hope of Jesus Christ. Hold your head up high, and keep fighting. Victory is on the way! Let us have that Job spirit: "though he slay me, yet will I trust in him: but I will maintain mine own ways before him" (Job 13:15). Job had the best of everything, but his "things" were taken away. The good news is that, in the end, he got more than double for his trouble. Rebuild me, Lord.

2
CHAPTER

Try Him Before You Deny Him

And David built there an altar unto the LORD,
and offered burnt offerings and peace offerings,
and called upon the LORD; and he answered
him from heaven by fire upon the altar of burnt
offering.

—1 Chronicles 21:26

Trials and tribulations are a part of life. We have all experienced times when we felt that we were down and out for the count. Sometimes our deliverance is seamless. Have you ever cried over a situation and then, some time later, you realize that you are not crying anymore but cannot even remember when you actually stopped crying? In such moments, all I can do is raise my hands and my voice and say "Thank you, Jesus!" Is there anything too hard for God? No!

I am a witness that God is a miracle worker. I have seen him do it time after time again, not only in my life but also in the lives of my closest friends and family. New mercies I see every day. My grandmother used to always say that "he'll make a way out of no way," and I have found that to be true. He is truly amazing.

We are so used to not-so-good things happening in our lives that, when the blessings come in like a flood, we never truly get to enjoy them because we are always thinking in the back of our minds, *This is too good to be true. Something not so good must be coming around the corner.* God is the father who desires to give good gifts to his children. We often sing the song "I'd rather have Jesus more than anything."

Someone once asked me, "How can you sing that? You've never been offered anything. You've never been sick and offered a cure. You've never been offered a billion dollars—which could ultimately get you out of debt and allow you to buy just about anything you want." Consider this; everything belongs to God. He can bless us with cures, riches, and anything else that we desire if we trust in and acknowledge him with all our heart. Let us have the same mindset as that of Paul. Let us be content in whatever situation we find ourselves in. That is a difficult thing to do when it seems that your world is crumbling right before your eyes. Because of our human nature, it is not easy to trust God. Trusting is a learned behavior, but you cannot learn if you do not study and apply.

I am a witness that sometimes he shows up even before you pray. Have you ever thought about something, and it came to pass even before you formed your lips to pray? Do not let your troubles get the best of you. Call on Jesus, and I guarantee that he will answer!

3

My Condition Is Not My Conclusion

> And Jesus looking upon them saith, With men it
> is impossible, but not with God: for with God all
> things are possible.
>
> —Mark 10:27

Like me, I am sure that you have found yourself in a situation where you simply could not see your way out but, by the grace of God, you made it out in one piece. You did not lose your life or your mind. We can save ourselves from a lot of stress and worry if we will only put it in God's hands and ride it out! I know that, beyond a doubt, no matter how bad things may seem today, tomorrow will be a brighter day. Weeping may endure for a night, but joy will come in the morning. We are so blessed and often do not realize how blessed we are. With each day, we are guaranteed a new set of mercies and joy. Who can ask for more? My advice to you and to myself is to not be fooled or confused by what we see in front of us. Wait until the dust settles. Only then will we be able to see the picture more clearly—what awaits us.

There was a time in my life when everything was bad—my credit, my attitude, and the decisions that I made. But when I truly came to my senses and recalled everything that my mother had taught me and all the principles that I read and learned about in the Bible and started applying those things to my everyday walk, that was when things took a turn for the better. We cannot stand on the things that others say about us, but we can stand on what God says about us. Values like believers having been justified and redeemed, us having been accepted by Christ, us having been blessed with every spiritual blessing in heavenly places, and the peace of God guarding our hearts and minds. Values like God supplying all our needs and, in Christ, us having wisdom, righteousness, sanctification, and redemption.

Until I became good and grown, I used to struggle with not being pretty enough, good enough, or smart enough. Even today, some may say that I am very competitive or overcompensate for things (do/doing too much). It is none of those things. I have to admit that I am borderline perfectionist, I am a visionary, and I love to succeed! I truly believe that I accomplish anything that I set my head, heart, hands, and heels to do. No one can convince me otherwise. My father always told his children that, if you start it, you should, can, and will finish it. My mother, on the other hand, told us that she was not that concerned about what we wanted to become, *but* whatever we decided to be, just be the best at it. Both of these instructions have stayed with me throughout childhood and now into adulthood.

I have come to accept who I am and who I am not. I love life and all the things it has to offer. It is not easy being me, but I am mastering the trade. I just strive to be my best, do my best, and help others to do the same. If I have it, I will share it. I am happier now than I have ever been. How did I get to this space? I learned not to take myself so seriously. I used to force myself to smile, but now, as soon as the Lord allows my eyes to open each morning, I start at one hundred. I realize that I am better than blessed. And my grandma was right: "The more you give, the more he will give to you." I am fearfully and wonderfully made. Hallelujah!

4

The Numbers Don't Add Up

> And he commanded the multitude to sit down on the grass, and took the five loaves, and the two fishes, and looking up to heaven, he blessed, and brake, and gave the loaves to his disciples, and the disciples to the multitude. And they did all eat, and were filled: and they took up of the fragments that remained twelve baskets full. And they that had eaten were about five thousand men, beside women and children.
> —Matthew 14:19–21

As I look back on my life and recall the times when I had to choose between rent and other things, I can also recall how God carried me through, how he took my one hundred dollars and made it stretch as if it were one thousand dollars. Can I get a witness? There were times when I was literally down to my last dollar. I would ask myself, "How am I going to make it?" And before I could formulate that thought into a prayer, God had already answered. By the time I got home to my mailbox, an unexpected refund or rebate check would be there patiently waiting for me. It is at those times when I would hear a still, small voice saying "Just ask and believe." Thank you, Jesus!

There have been times when I would write a check and ask God this: "Lord, I am writing this check to keep my electric supply on, and I pray that, by the time this check reaches the bank, you would have made a way." Now I have to be careful to thank him every day because the provisions are there, and sometimes, when he blesses us, we tend to forget those times when we truly had to walk by faith and not by sight. In all things, I give thanks. As he has blessed me, it is my duty to bless others, not looking for anything in return from those whom God allows me to bless.

Though my "earthly" bank account does not look like it now, I am patiently awaiting the day when I will be able to bless my church big-time beyond all that I can ask or think. Oh, that day is coming! My hands will touch it because my heart is in it!

My blessings have moved from the tens to the hundreds and, recently, to the thousands. I am headed for the tens of thousands and then on to the hundreds of thousands. I can see the millions. You know how your car side-view mirror has that "Objects may be closer than they appear" message? It may be far off, but I can see it, and I believe that it is nearer than I think it is. Some may say that I have a vivid imagination, but what is vivid can also be real.

5

CHAPTER

We Can't Work It Out

And whosoever will not receive you, when ye go
out of that city, shake off the very dust from your
feet for a testimony against them.

—Luke 9:5

Some relationships are seasonal or are just not meant to be. We tend to hold on to "dead" things. Of course, after you have nurtured, you have to give it time to grow. But if it does not bring life, at some point, you have to be willing to let go. I have come to know that there have been times when God desired that I have more, better, but because my hands were already full of things that he did not ordain, I could not accept all that he had for me. I am so much better at letting go now.

I used to be in a relationship with someone I loved with everything that I had and some things that were not mine to give. I knew in my gut that this was not right or healthy, but my heart had a different opinion. If someone tells you to trust your heart, you better pray until your answer comes, because your heart can and will play tricks on you. Even though I try to convince myself to let it go, there are times when the *good times*—though there were few—cross my mind, but then I come to myself and remember the *not-so-good times*. After this relationship, it took me nearly a decade to regain my composure, and I get frustrated at myself at times for having taken so long to heal, and I have to make myself believe that it was all part of what made me who I am today.

Most people want "instant"—just add water and stir—but sometimes, you have to preheat the oven at 350 degrees, mix, flour the pan, and bake for forty-five minutes. Some folks think that I am timid. It's not that at all. I have learned to be extremely careful with where I direct my attention. Some things simply are not worth my time and attention. Some battles are not mine. I may be slow to start, but I am sure to finish. When I say that I am done, you can believe it. Above all else, I choose to be happy.

Now, when things do not go the way that I think they should, I sit back and enjoy the ride because I know that, at some point, the roller coaster will stop, and I will get off. My curls may be a little out of place due to the wind, but my feet will be on solid ground. You have to learn to steady yourself and KIM (keep it moving). It is not so bad to experience situations that take your breath away; just make sure that you are not being smothered. Every problem isn't yours to solve. I give my problems to Jesus. He is the master at subtraction, addition, multiplication, and division!

6

CHAPTER

Calling All Angels

For he shall give his angels charge over thee, to
keep thee in all thy ways.

—Psalm 91:11

I have lost some things in my life that were very special to me.
More important than things, I have lost some very important people. I was fortunate enough to be blessed with a wonderful maternal uncle and aunts. Over the years, I have had four maternal aunts
who passed away—two suddenly and two from cancer. I also lost my
father due to cancer. Please believe me when I say that the core of my
essence was shaken and is still rocking. I know that scars do not heal
overnight and that, day by day, the intensity of the pain will subside.
I look forward to the day when I can move from under the cloud of
sadness. I have to constantly remind myself that the joy of the Lord
is my strength, that his strength is made perfect in my weakness, and
that weeping may endure for a night but joy will come in the morning. I thank God for his grace, his mercy (new set every morning),
and his favor. Without them, I do not know how I can survive or
where I would be, and for that, I am so grateful.

It is so important to love those you say that you love. Never
let too much time pass between visits, phone calls, letters, or even
disagreements. Resolve conflict quickly as we never know what our
last words to a person will be. Be genuinely nice to people, and smile.
You never know who may be watching, and one act of kindness may
just save someone's life.

We have to meet people where they are and realize that no one is perfect—not even you or me. Thank God for the angels that he has assigned to us for protection. Sometimes our attitudes and actions are not godly, but he still loves and cares for us. We should have that same attitude toward people we think have done us wrong, stabbed us in the back, et cetera. I am sure that others can say the same about us. I am reminded of the passage of scripture in Ecclesiastes 7:21–22: "Also take no heed unto all words that are spoken; lest thou hear thy servant curse thee: For oftentimes also thine own heart knoweth that thou thyself likewise hast cursed others."

I will be the first to admit that I need help with controlling my words, actions, and thoughts. That is my prayer every morning and throughout the day: "Lord set guard over my mouth, be a door unto my lips, help me to be gracious in speech, help me to give soft answers, and teach me how to answer every man."

Words can kill, and they can rebuild. I choose to rebuild. It does not cost anything except for a moment of your time (the time that God has graciously given) to uplift someone's spirit. There are times when you will be tested. That is the time to call all angels to help you to get through this thing called life. Angels, angels, where are you? "Right here where we have always been."

7

To Get One, Be One

And I will bless them that bless thee, and curse him that curseth thee: and in thee shall all families of the earth be blessed.

—Genesis 12:3

I have heard all my life that God has a plan for my life. I used to run around trying to figure out what the purpose of my life was. Then, at a Tuesday-night Bible study, I received the revelation, and though I had read and heard it numerous times, suddenly the light came on. "Let us hear the conclusion of the whole matter: Fear God, and keep His commandments: for this is the whole duty of man" (Ecclesiastes 12:13).

All I have ever wanted to do in life—maybe not all that I ever wanted but certainly one of the main things—was to be a blessing to others and take care of my family. Simple. That is it. I have learned that, if I take care of myself (spiritually, personally, financially, and socially) and others, I can step back and watch God do the rest. Do not get me wrong. You have to put your work in, but when God sees you climbing, he will give you a boost!

As long as he wakes me up every morning on this side of the land of the living, I will bless him at all times, and I will bless somebody else! I want to be a storehouse. Not that God needs help, but I aim to please him and want to be just like him! I am blessed to be a blessing!

8

CHAPTER

A Way With Words

A soft answer turneth away wrath: but grievous
words stir up anger.

—Proverbs 15:1

Have you ever had a conversation with someone and, before
you began the conversation, you were happy and cheerful but, by
the end of the conversation, you wanted to shake some sense into the
person that you were talking with? No, I do not advocate violence,
but I am just expressing my feelings. I have learned that some people
are just plain miserable. I really do not understand how this can be.
As I look at the stars, the sun, the moon, and everything that God
has given us, I cannot be depressed or ungrateful. As I mentioned
before, I am so thankful God sees fit to wake me each morning. Not
only that, but with the dawning of each new day, he gifts me with a
new set of mercies.

I have learned (the hard way) that sometimes your friends are
really not your friends. There are those who will dislike you no matter what. You try your very best to appease or please using soft, sweet
words and actions and reactions but to no avail. The sad thing is that
sometimes you do not even know why they dislike you. Could it be
jealousy or envy? What can you really say to a person that will make
them feel differently about you, especially when their main goal in
life is to make your life miserable? Because misery loves company,
but I do not feel up to having visitors today. Well, you keep giving
soft answers, and you ask God to set guard over your mouth and

your tongue. I say this because, from my own experience, no matter how "spiritual" you claim and want to be, the "human" side rears its head every now and then. It may be a bit challenging to continue speaking pleasant words to someone whose sole purpose in life is to see how deep they can cut you and how much you will bleed. In all things, you have to constantly remind yourself that your words do weigh a lot. Stay in a state of repentance, love those who do not love you, and always remember the words that will pretty much help you to overcome any obstacle or distraction: "God bless," "God forgive," and "Go in peace."

I am learning to crucify my flesh. It takes an enormous amount of time and effort to do so. Crucifixion hurts, but it is worth it! Every day, every second of the day, you have to train your heart and mind in the way of Philippians 4:8: "Whatsoever things are true, whatsoever things are honest, whatsoever things just, whatsoever things are pure, whatsoever things are lovely, whatsoever things are of a good report...think on these things."

9

CHAPTER

You Can't Tell Everybody Everything

> But thou, when thou prayest, enter into thy
> closet, and when thou hast shut thy door, pray
> to thy Father which is in secret; and thy Father
> which seeth in secret shall reward thee openly.
> —Matthew 6:6

I have loss a grandmother and four maternal aunts over the years. This has left a void in my heart and life and the lives of my family members. As for me, each day I try to fill this hole with great memories. Some make me laugh, and some cause me to cry happy tears. I am not certain of what tomorrow may bring, but I know, without a doubt, that my family and I will keep praying, hoping, and trusting, and we will prevail. Not one day goes by when I do not think of them. The first aunt who passed away helped to ignite the creativity in me. The second helped me to truly understand the power and rewards of having a solid relationship with Jesus Christ. When I look back on my life and see all that I have accomplished through the grace of God, I realize that I am blessed to bless others. So the sternness and strictness that my fourth aunt who passed away wore like a garment no longer seems harsh but necessary. Without it, I do not know where I would be. Actually, I have an idea, but thank God that it did not turn out that way. My third aunt that passed away was my heart—I was her daughter.

My grandmother was a charm, and she did not play games with her grandchildren. When she said something, she meant it, and believe me when I say that she did not spare the rod. She had the ability to look into our eyes and know if we were telling the truth or not. Woe unto the one who spoke a lie! The thing that I remember the most is that she always made certain that we were clean and fed and that we respected our elders, within and outside the church walls. She was classy and was always adorned with a fancy hat with a matching cape when she attended church. Sometimes we fail to realize just how much someone means to us until they are gone. It is so important, like my grandmother used to say, to give people their flowers while they are living. Proverbs 27:5 tells us that "open rebuke is better than hidden love." Love is not only an emotion; it is also an action word. I made a commitment to myself to be more mindful with regard to putting my love into action.

My grandmother also taught us not to be blabbermouths. If you are always talking, then it may be difficult to hear. Be careful whom you disclose you innermost secrets to. Everyone who claims to be your "friend" may not have your best interest at heart.

There are some things that you should not take to anyone but Jesus. Remember the songs "Take It to the Lord in Prayer" and "What a Friend We Have in Jesus"? I have learned to take everything to him in prayer—my struggles and my accomplishments (through his grace), my fears and my fierceness, my moments of faintness and my triumphs, and everything else.

10

Dress For Success

> Wherefore take unto you the whole armour of
> God, that ye may be able to withstand in the evil
> day, and having done all, to stand.
> —Ephesians 6:13

I used to wear any brand, but I now only wear designer gear. My designer of choice is "God's" best. It is essential that believers look good both inside and out. Have you ever met someone who looked as if they just wandered out of a high-class magazine but, when they opened their mouth and spoke, all you heard or felt was pure evil? After they spoke, though they did not change clothes, they did not appear to be so fabulous after all. That goes to show you that it is not enough to be *dressed to kill* but that you are also *dressed to live*. What you wear on the inside does make the difference, and what is truly inside you will come out at one point or another.

The Bible instructs us to have our loins girded about with truth, have on the breastplate of righteousness, have our feet shod with the preparation of the gospel of peace, and to take the shield of faith, the helmet of salvation, and the sword of the spirit. If one is not dressed with these, then they are not *dressed to live*. My daily prayer is that God would allow his light to shine all around me and through me so that others may see his light. My desire is to be a magnet, attracting others to Christ. I would never ever want anyone to walk away from me thinking or saying to themselves or others, "She is dressed to kill." I work extremely hard at making others feel special and worth it. There are times when you have to have on a pair of good walking shoes too. There are some—regardless of how much you have given or how hard you have tried to build and maintain a good relationship—who will stab you in the chest. Those are the times when you have to not stab them back but to love them from a distance.

Keep on loving, but keep on walking, as well. It has been my experience that, if you remain in that environment for too long, you risk the chance of your clothes getting dirty, because there are some, when they see the light, who will do all that is within their power to put that light out. One has to be careful to always be dressed, because the enemy comes in all shapes, colors, and sizes as he is the master of disguises. We have to outdress him; that's for sure.

11
CHAPTER

Don't Faint

But they that wait upon the LORD shall renew their strength; they shall mount up with wings as eagles; they shall run, and not be weary; and they shall walk, and not faint.

—Isaiah 40:31

My mother always taught me, in whatever I find my heart and hands to do, to do those things to the best of my ability. To win the prize, you have to be in the race. Though there have been times when *great* things seem to have fallen on my lap with no effort, I do believe that faith without works is dead. There are times when your faith kicks in only at the point when you throw your hands up and say "Whatever, Lord."

In this life, every day cannot be peaches and cream. Some days, you are going to have to take the sour cream and onion. But always remember, no matter how heavy the load, keep walking, and keep moving. At some point, you will reach the finish line.

The race is not given to the swift or to the strong but to the one who endures to the end. Sadly, many of us will not reach the finish line because we get distracted or discouraged. I know that it gets rough, but you have to stay focused and keep it moving.

I know, without a doubt, that my strength will forever be renewed because I will wait upon the Lord. He promised never to leave or forsake, and he is a god who keeps his promises. Can I get a witness?

I have made up in my mind that, as long as God wakes me each day, he will equip me to do those things that are assigned to my head, heart, and hands to do. There are times when you know, without a doubt, that it had to be God because you did not have the will or strength to do all that was needed to be done. As long as he continues to wake me, I will try my best to walk in his will and his way. He gives us the gift, so the least we can do is give him the glory. Amen again!

12

CHAPTER

Before I Let Go

And when he saw that he prevailed not against him, he touched the hollow of his thigh; and the hollow of Jacob's thigh was out of joint, as he wrestled with him.

And he said, Let me go, for the day breaketh. And he said, I will not let thee go, except thou bless me.

—Genesis 32:25–26

Life is like a roller-coaster ride in many ways. You enter the carnival for one purpose only, and that is to have fun. The line for the roller coaster is always the longest. You stand there thinking to yourself, *I must be crazy to stand here*, but you stand there anyway waiting for your turn. The custodian tells you to tie down and to hold on. This is after he measures to determine if you are tall enough for the ride. So you take a seat, secure the safety bar, and attempt to secure any loose items. *Good job*, so you think. Then it is slow moving to the top. Once at the top, you sit for a moment, and fear and anxiety often get the best of you. You ask yourself, "What have I gotten myself into?" At that moment, you begin an adventure like no other. A quick drop, a sharp turn, and a jerk here and a jerk there make you feel like your heart will beat out of your chest, not to mention how your stomach feels. Some lose their jewelry, hair, purse, etc. Didn't the custodian instruct you to secure all loose items? Finally, the ride ends, and you say that you will never do that again, but what do you know? Back in line again. "This time, I am going to conquer it." No fear!

Such is life. There will be times when your faith is tested. Quizzes you can deal with because they only count for a minute percentage of your final grade. Maybe it is me, but have you ever studied for a test and, in the nervousness of it all, you seem to have forgotten what you studied?

You sit for a moment and pray that all that you have studied comes to your remembrance. You are on a roll. It is all coming back to you now. Then you run into a question or situation that knocks you to your knees. Like being on the roller-coaster ride, you lose things and people who are very valuable to you. Your first instinct is to quit—to give up. You get so fed up with the twists and turns, the jerks, the heartaches, the things that make your stomach clinch.

You pray, and God answers, and you are ready to get back on the ride. Why? Because it was all worth it. I am better, stronger, and more courageous—always paying attention. I am still working on me. Working on not always wanting things my way. Above all, I want things God's way! My way will fail, but God's way will last. I am learning more and more each day to consult with God first about what he wants and expects of me each day. I then tell him of my personal feelings and plans but end our first daily session with "Okay, God, whatever you want, I'll do. It's you and me reaching lost souls, offering love and words of encouragement to those who need it the most…let's do this!"

13

Faith Don't Fail Me Now

Let us hold fast to profession of our faith without
wavering; (for he is faithful that promised;).
—Hebrews 10:23

Really, I am just a simple girl who is somewhat complicated.
The next decade of my life is quickly approaching, and I must
redeem the time. I have been endowed by the Creator with many
gifts and talents. With my main focus in life being geared toward
encouraging, empowering, and enriching the lives of others, I have
neglected to apply these principles to my own life. The fear of failing
plays a major part. I want to grow boldness and courage to walk into
my destiny and not let fear intimidate me. I have decided that fear
will no longer hold me hostage. My faith will be the shield to protect
me from fear, doubt, and defeat.

Though I am writing this now, my feet seem to still be stuck to
the floor, but I will continue to speak "victory," believing that it will
come to pass. For from this point moving forward, I will not focus
on the obstacles or problems but will instead focus on the promises.
My life does have purpose, and I must fulfill my destiny. No longer
will I let naysayers make me feel that I am not good enough, smart
enough, pretty enough—enough is enough. God has already instilled
within me all that I will or can ever need to get through this thing
called life. I am everything that he has called me to be. I thank him
for my faith most of all. I know that he is a god who can do anything
and all things, but there are times when the enemy's breath is so hot

on my neck that it shakes my faith. It is at those times that I pray, "Lord, help my unbelief." He is an on-time god! I am destined to finish strong.

We are both natural and spiritual, and there will be times when your faith is tested. Trials come to build your faith. A bodybuilder does not wake up one morning and say "I want muscles" and expect them to magically appear. No. He draws out a plan, sets his goals and milestones, celebrates his victories, and does not dwell on his shortcomings. He keeps working, stays focused, and before he knows it, one day, he will awaken, and his dream would have been fulfilled. What is the purpose of obstacles, anyway? Obstacles are not so bad. They build your stamina and self-confidence (when you overcome them).

14

CHAPTER

Safety In The Ark

> And every living substance was destroyed which was upon the face of the ground, both man, and cattle, and the creeping things, and the fowl of the heaven; and they were destroyed from the earth: and Noah only remained alive, and they that were with him in the ark.
>
> —Genesis 7:23

I know that you have run into one or two situations in your life that would have destroyed most, but you are still here. The fact that you are still here is not by accident. You have found the key to survival. You cannot let distractions trick, trap, or trouble you. You have to keep it moving! Misery, depression, and things along those lines can be refunded. Better yet, do not even buy them! When the enemy gives you his sales pitch, just tell him that what he is selling is not worth it.

Sometimes we measure our success by the stuff that we have around us. I do declare that it is the stuff that is within us, not the stuff around us, that allows us to be the light in an otherwise-dark place. We should be like Noah and be satisfied with what we can carry. Leave all the unnecessary stuff behind. The extra baggage may kill you.

I do not know about you, but I need God to empty me of some things and fill me with his glory. Empty me of stress and worry, unforgiveness, anxiety, depression, low self-esteem, bitterness, boastfulness, among other things. When everything around me dies, I will live!

It took me years to learn this lesson. I have heard it all my life, but I truly adopted it when I joined and became an active member of the Ark of Safety Christian Church. I did not know that life could be so good. Yes, I read and studied the Bible, prayed, and did all the other things that Christians should do. It is at the Ark of Safety Christian Church where I truly began to understand the difference between relationship and religion. You can rent a room at the church, but until you build that intimacy between you and God—that we love each other and we are going to stay together and take care of our relationship with each other—you will never understand the principle and practice of abundant living. Yes, life is good!

I am not as uptight as I used to be. When you learn to trust and lean on God, you will enter a state of peacefulness that I cannot even explain. You will have that type of peace and confidence with which you can look the enemy dead in his eye and command that he go back to hell. You have to keep an eye on him, though, because he has accumulated a bunch of frequent-flyer miles.

15

Who Can I Run To?

In all your ways acknowledge him, and he will
direct thy paths.

—Proverbs 3:6

My grandmother used to say, "If you have not seen rain in your
life, wait awhile." Some may think that, once you receive salvation
and begin to walk in Christianity, not-so-good things will not hap-
pen to you. Quite the contrary. As I began to study the Word of
God, I discovered scripture that speaks of his promises of protection,
promises of provision, promises of victory, promises of guidance, and
promises of forgiveness, among other promises. So I ask myself, why
would he make such promises? He made them because he knew that
receiving salvation and operating in Christianity will only enrage the
adversary, but he wanted to make sure that we, as believers, know
that he is a present help in the time of need and that he will not put
more on us than we can bear. To that, I say, "Let it rain!" I will trust
him even when I cannot trace him, for he is a promise keeper! I thank
him for his peace, which is perfect; his grace, which is amazing and
sufficient; and his mercy, which endureth forever. We are all human,
and we all make mistakes. Get up, get over it, and keep it moving!
Jesus does not ever have to worry about me being down too long.
I may stumble and fall, but rest assured, he does not have to worry
about me staying in that condition. I will get up and catch up! When
the enemy comes in like a flood, you cannot walk or run. You have
to swim or float!

I have learned to seek him in all things. There are times when I did not consult him first, and I cannot tell you how much trouble, dilemma, and stress I found myself in. I have learned to listen to that still, small voice. It has never led me astray. You have to talk to him on a regular basis and build a strong relationship. You need to talk to him regularly so you can know his voice. My hope, faith, and trust lie in him. He knows it because I remind him of this every day. I am working on strengthening our relationship because I want him to be able to trust me with anything too. I tell him every day how much I love and adore him. I thank him for everything! For the very air that he allows me to breathe; the flowers, shrubs, and trees; the animals; the sun, moon, and stars. I am so thankful that he has given me dominion and truly appreciate him allowing me to occupy his great space. Lord, please take this stubborn head, hard heart, and tainted hands, and mold me over again. Yes, I will always acknowledge him and will stand on the promise that he will direct my path! Lord, I thank you for my life—every loss, every victory, every tear, every smile, for every time that I stumbled and fell, but you allowed me to get up, dust myself off, and carry on! Thank you, God, for your peace, protection, provision, and your patience!

16

CHAPTER

Forgive Or Relive

For if ye forgive men their trespasses, your heavenly Father will also forgive you.

—Matthew 6:14

We have all experienced some sort of hurt in life. There are times when this hurt is self-inflicted. We tend to wear our heart on our sleeve and are offended by the least thing. Eventually, we come to the realization that people matter always but that some of their issues, though they are worth much to that individual, should not clutter your personal space. The smartest or most peaceful people are those who have the ability to tune out or avoid the noise. Do not let other people's words or actions, particularly the negative ones, cloud your heart or your mind. There are some, God help them, who are mean and bitter. I dare not say that they are that way naturally, because they were not born that way. Such may live to inflict pain and hurt on others. Have you ever encountered someone and wondered to yourself, *Why are they so mean?* So the question becomes "How does one react to such a person?" My grandmother used to say, "Kill them with kindness!"

When people offend you in any way, you have to practice and learn *forgiveness* and then move on. We tend to say "I forgive you," but forgiveness is an action word. You say it with your mouth, but you have to say it with your heart, as well. Personally, I had to learn to release the hurt. It did not come easy; it was and is a process. I pray daily for the Lord to forgive me and empty me of all unforgiveness that I may be harboring, consciously or subconsciously. With that, how can I ask him for forgiveness if I am unwilling to do the same? Forgive with your heart, mind, and soul, and keep it moving! Do not find yourself stuck; move past the hurt and disappointment. Learn to forgive yourself, and let go of the regrets. Then and only then will you be able to love and live wholeheartedly. Time is too valuable to waste or lose. Cut down on some of the stress and anxiety. Let it go and live!

17

Prayer Still Works

And it shall come to pass, that before they call,
I will answer; and while they are yet speaking, I
will hear.

—Isaiah 65:24

I love to pray, and I love to listen to others pray, as well. There were times when I would listen to others pray and desire to pray like them. Everything seemed to flow, and they were so eloquent and knew the right words to say. Then I came to learn that God looks at the heart and all he wants you to do is to come into his presence in spirit and in truth with thanksgiving. You do not get extra credit based on the number of words you speak. God looks at the purity of your heart and your intentions.

Even as a child, I prayed at least twice a day: in the morning, when I awakened, not by my own might but by the grace of God, and at night, before I lay down to sleep. As I grew in my walk with God, my prayers became more intentional. My routine "I want" prayers evolved into "Lord, I thank you" prayers. How and what one prays for make a difference. Thank God for the Holy Spirit, which intercedes on my behalf. There are times when I get the unction to pray but my thoughts and words escape me. At these times, I lift my eyes to the hills from whence cometh my help and utter, "Lord, have mercy." The truth is that God knows what you stand in the need of even before you need it and even before you ask. Prayer is very powerful. As humans, it is only natural that we desire things that we need and things that we want, but sometimes, we need to cease from asking and start praising and giving thanks for what we already have. I thank God for the privilege of prayer. Prayer combined with faith makes the impossible possible. This tool had been proven to tear down strong holds, tunnel through mountains, make jagged edges smooth, and to bring about peace and contentment even in the midst of a storm.

We often pray to God concerning our personal plan for our life, but our prayer should be "God, reveal your plan for my life to me." He knew our end before our beginning. So of course, he knows every bang and bump and in and out. Our blessings are calculated down to the point and penny. He knows! I work constantly but also make time to rest. Sometimes I place "rest" events on my calendar. Believe it or not, most of my most creative and concrete thoughts and ideas come to me while I am asleep. I may be struggling with a difficult issue during the day, but I refuse to take such issues with me into the sleep realm. When I lie down, it is in peace and in sleep. I give all my unresolved issues to God at night, and believe me, by the time God awakens me the next morning, he has dropped a resolution into my spirit. Regardless of what you are going through, take your burdens to the Lord, and leave them there!

18

Keep The Testimony

If thy children will keep my covenant and my
testimony that I shall teach them, their children
shall also sit upon thy throne for evermore.
—Psalm 132:12

In all things, give thanks as they could have been worse. No
matter how bad off you think you are, there is always someone who
will not hesitate to change places with you. I have been on cloud
eighteen (nine plus nine) for some time now.

Not too long ago, I witnessed a miracle that I know could have
only come from God Almighty. My grandson graduated elementary
and middle school and now in high school. I guess you are wonder-
ing what is so magnificent or extraordinary about that. Well, he was
diagnosed with autism at the age of three and did not talk until he
was about five years old. He attended an elementary school that was
a neighborhood school but had an extraordinary special education
program. Would you believe that he gave an opening address to all
the students, parents, and guests? His speech went like this:

> Welcome everybody. My name is _____. Would
> you believe that I have a dream? If you have a
> dream, you have to protect it. When I came to
> Panorama Elementary School, I did not talk
> much. No one can do everything, but everyone
> can do something. Never let anyone tell you,

you cannot do something. You can do anything
if you believe in yourself. Today I can! I can say
and read this speech. Today I am my dream come
true. Dare to dream!

When I say that all the students, parents, workers, and guests
were in tears, believe it! About a week before his graduation, he con-
tinually asked about a graduation cap. We brought a cap to school,
and his teacher allowed him to wear it during his speech. He delivered
that speech with so much poise and conviction that his great-grand-
mother was about to ignite a praise-and-worship service in that audi-
torium. Hold your mule, Mama.

We have always prayed for deliverance but did not expect this—
at least not at this magnitude. Dear God, help my unbelief. God
is more than amazing! Just believe that, no matter how dark today
may seem, tomorrow will be a brighter day! We will forever hold this
testimony in our hearts and tell others about the goodness and faith-
fulness of God. If you only knew how we labored on our knees and
in our hearts. Prayer works, and I am so thankful for the privilege of
being able to bow before a sin-forgiving, soul-saving, life-changing,
miracle-working, prayer-answering God. Like my grandmother used
to say, "You do not know, like I know, what he has done for me." I
give God all praise, honor, and glory, not only for the things that he
has done but because of who he is—awesome in power, amazing,
magnificent, mighty, wonderful, glorious, victorious, and indescrib-
able. Hallelujah and amen!

19

CHAPTER

Attitude Of Gratitude

Enter into his gates with thanksgiving, and into his courts with praise: be thankful unto him, and bless his name.

—Psalm 100:4

My father recently went home to be with the Lord. Though I am sad to see him go, I am thankful for the eighty years that God allowed him to walk this earth. He was diagnosed with that dreadful *C* disease (do not even say its name) that has plagued so many and have us looking forward to the day that we can declare "Cured!" When he was first diagnosed at the age of seventy-five, we prayed and asked God for more time. Our prayers were answered, and we were given five more years. Is not that a blessing? We were able to celebrate his eightieth birthday, but he passed away six days later. In my daily prayers, I thanked God for the lives of my mother and my father and asked that he renew their health and strength. I do believe that my father's health and strength were renewed, and I thank God that he was saved. So yes, we mourn, but not as those who have no hope. In all things, I do give thanks!

My father taught us so many things. He taught us to soar and not to settle. He taught us to tend to our own business and not to meddle in the affairs of others. He taught us the importance of having a good heart, a sound mind, and clean hands. He also taught us to fight and helped us to realize that some things are not worth fighting for. I was taught the strategy of taking something negative and reforming it into something positive and not to wear my feelings on my sleeve. I truly thank God that he has blessed me abundantly. I look for others to bless, and it seems, that the more I pour out, the more blessings come in. That is how successful living works. You teach your children and teach them to teach their children. Talk to them even when they do not want to listen. Teach them to be appreciative and to respect others. God still talks to me even in my sleep. You cannot beat God's giving. If you figure God in, he will figure it (whatever it is) out.

When I look back on my life, there are times when I do not know how I made it through. Then I came to realize that it was no power of my own but of God. I thank him for our relationship. He is reliable. Even when I go astray, he cares and has always cared enough that he assigned Secret Service agents (angels) to me. Yes, I am enrolled in the Witness Protection Program (WPP). No weapon formed against me will prosper, and for that, I am so thankful. I have conditioned my mind and my mouth so that I will not become my own worst enemy, nor will I tear down anyone else with my mouth, my thoughts, or my actions. I bless God always, and for those times when I may fall short, I thank God for the Holy Spirit, which intercedes on my behalf!

20
CHAPTER

What's Next?

But as it is written, Eye hath not seen, nor ear heard, neither have entered into the heart of man, the things which God hath prepared for them that love him.

—1 Corinthians 2:9

I have established goals and developed a plan. All I have to do now is to get to work. The walls and fences have been torn down, doors have been unlocked and opened, the gifts have been stirred up, and by the mercy and grace of God, all things are possible. My desire is to stay focused, be constant in prayer, to always be in a thankful state, and to no longer look at roadblocks as obstacles, but as opportunities. We are creatures of habit. We tend to take the same route with hopes of new scenery. Roadblocks force us to take a different route. A different route, though it may be challenging, helps to ignite our critical/strategic thinking, builds our muscle, and helps us to discover new or different things and people. I am ecstatic about the future! Not only in heaven but also about what is in store right here on earth. I will always pass the blessings on to others. I can wait awhile for my wings. In the meantime, I may work toward gaining my pilot license.

I want to and will do more work in my church and the community, increase my daily prayer and devotion, keep cutting away at negativity, be more of a positive, godly influence in my own life and in the lives of others, and simply keep it moving. I choose to live an abundant life! I am trusting that the Holy Spirit will lead, guide, comfort, strengthen, and protect me. I also choose to be happy and understand that happiness is not a destination; it is a lifestyle. I look forward to speaking with you again…soon.

About the Author

Evangela C. W. Jeffrey is a native of Washington, DC, and currently resides in Maryland. She loves to sew, knit, and crochet and read Christian fiction, poetry, and the Holy Bible. She also dabbles in acting, arts and crafts, gardening, event planning, and interior decorating. Evangela is known for giving her time, talent, and treasure to help make life better for other people—a philanthropist of sorts. Her personal mantra is F6: faith, favor, family, friends, finance, and forgiveness. This book, *Calculated Blessings: Every Tear Counts*, tells of her triumph and testimony in all the F6! To those who are wearing the uniform of hurt, disappointment, or shame, wipe your tears, and change your clothes! God knows, and he cares!